choose once again

Selections from
A Course in Miracles

Foundation for Inner Peace

Edited by Julius J. Finegold and William N. Thetford

Celestial Arts • Berkeley, California

Celestial Arts
P.O. Box 7327
Berkeley, California 94707

First Printing, April 1981

Manufactured in the United States of America

Library of Congress Cataloging in Publication Data
Main entry under title:

Choose once again.

1. Foundation for Inner Peace. I. Thetford, William N.
II. Finegold, Julius J. III. Foundation for Inner Peace.
IV. Foundation for Inner Peace. A course in miracles.
BX9998.C52   230'.99   80-28828
ISBN: 089087-413-1

14 15 16 17 — 01 00 99 98 97

Dedicated to
Helen Schucman
1909 – 1981

This book is presented in the hope that it will enable the reader to experience miracles—those shifts in perception which remove the blocks to the awareness of love's presence in our lives.

introduction "Teach only love, for that is what you are" is an expression of our true function and reality. As we begin to awaken from our dream of separation, we recognize that not only is this true but also that there is nothing else we need or could possibly desire except love. Our reality as love is the basic theme of *A Course in Miracles,* the work from which all of the passages in this book have been selected. Although much of *A Course in Miracles* is in blank verse, it is printed almost entirely in prose form. Verse form is used throughout this compilation of selections to highlight the beauty of language which illuminates the concepts presented.

What is *A Course in Miracles?* On one level, it is a 622-page *Text* which discusses theoretical concepts, a *Workbook for Students* containing 365 daily lessons designed for practical application of the concepts, and an 88-page *Manual for Teachers* which defines the role of teachers (all of us, as we are all teachers and pupils to each other). At another level, the *Course* is a reteaching of eternal truths, presented as a self-study course for personal transformation. It is a spiritual teaching, not a religion. It uses Christian terminology, but is ecumenical in nature, and states: "A universal theology is impossible, but a universal experience is not only possible but necessary."

1

One of the basic premises of the *Course* is that we live in a world of duality, of perception and knowledge, of appearance and reality. Knowledge is truth under one law—the law of love or God. The world of perception is the world of time, of change, of beginnings and endings. It is based on our interpretation, not on fact. It is a world of birth and death, founded on our belief in separation, scarcity, sin, guilt and fear. It is learned rather than given, unstable in its functioning, selective in its perceptual emphases and inaccurate in its interpretations. The world of knowledge, on the other hand, is the world of unity, abundance, sinlessness, love and eternal life.

Two distinct thought systems follow from the worlds of knowledge and perception. What we see and hear appear to be real because the mind permits into awareness only what conforms to our wishes. This leads us to a world of illusion, which needs constant defense because it is not real. It also leads us to thoughts of "sin," guilt about our "sins," and fear of punishment for them. Actually sin is simply a lack of love, a mistake or error calling for correction, not for guilt and pinishment.

Once we are caught in the world of perception we are caught in a dream, a dream of hell. In order to awaken to reality, recognizing Heaven as our true home, it is necessary to reverse our thinking and unlearn our mistakes. Forgiveness, the letting go of our belief in the reality of sin and guilt, is the primary means for bringing this thought reversal about. We must learn to forgive, not because we are being "good" and "charitable," but because what we are seeing is not true. By forgiving ourselves and others, we reaffirm the truth of our shared spiritual reality.

The aim of *A Course in Miracles* is to lead us from duality to oneness—to the realization of our At-one-ment with God, our Self and all people—our brothers. In this healing is our Salvation—we are *saved* from our misperception of ourselves as separated individuals. When our perception is corrected we remember our true or higher Self, created by God as His Son, and one with Christ. Salvation is really enlightenment, and enables us to accept the Christ within, and see with Christ's vision—love. To help us in attaining this goal we need to listen to God's Voice, the Holy Spirit, who serves as our inner guide. As the Epilogue of the *Workbook for Students* states: "Henceforth, hear but the Voice for God and for your Self . . . He will direct your efforts, telling you exactly what to do, how to direct your mind, and when to come to Him in silence, asking for His sure direction and His certain Word."

A Course in Miracles is published by the Foundation for Inner Peace, P.O. Box 635, Tiburon, California 94920.

Love, Which created me, is what I am.

*l*et us be still an instant, and forget
all things we ever learned, all thoughts we had,
and every preconception that we hold
of what things mean and what their purpose is.
Let us remember not our own ideas
of what the world is for. We do not know.
Let every image held of everyone
be loosened from our minds and swept away.

Be innocent of judgment, unaware
of any thoughts of evil or of good
that ever crossed your mind of anyone.
Now do you know him not. But you are free
to learn of him, and learn of him anew.
Now is he born again to you, and you
are born again to him, without the past
that sentenced him to die, and you with him.
Now is he free to live as you are free,
because an ancient learning passed away,
and left a place for truth to be reborn.

*t*he miracle comes quietly into
the mind that stops an instant and is still.
It reaches gently from that quiet time,
and from the mind it healed in quiet then,
to other minds to share its quietness.
And they will join in doing nothing to
prevent its radiant extension back
into the Mind Which caused all minds to be.
Born out of sharing, there can be no pause
in time to cause the miracle delay
in hastening to all unquiet minds,
and bringing them an instant's stillness, when
the memory of God returns to them.
Their own remembering is quiet now,
and what has come to take its place will not
be wholly unremembered afterwards.

*I rest in God today, and let Him work
in me and through me, while I rest in Him
in quiet and in perfect certainty.*

*t**he*** Thought of God created you. It left
you not, nor have you ever been apart
from it an instant. It belongs to you.
By it you live. It is your Source of life,
holding you one with it, and everything
is one with you because it left you not.
The Thought of God protects you, cares for you,
makes soft your resting place and smooth your way,
lighting your mind with happiness and love.
Eternity and everlasting life
shine in your mind, because the Thought of God
has left you not, and still abides with you.

*b**e*** in my mind, my Father, when I wake,
and shine on me throughout the day today.
Let every minute be a time in which
I dwell with You. And let me not forget
my hourly thanksgiving that You have
remained with me, and always will be there
to hear my call to You and answer me.
As evening comes, let all my thoughts be still
of You and of Your Love. And let me sleep
sure of my safety, certain of Your care,
and happily aware I am Your Son.

*g**od* is with me. He is my Source of life,
the life within, the air I breathe, the food
by which I am sustained, the water which
renews and cleanses me. He is my home,
wherein I live and move; the Spirit Which
directs my actions, offers me Its Thoughts,
and guarantees my safety from all pain.
He covers me with kindness and with care,
and holds in love the Son He shines upon,
who also shines on Him. How still is he
who knows the truth of what He speaks today!

od's Name can not be heard without response,
nor said without an echo in the mind
that calls you to remember. Say His Name,
and you invite the angels to surround
the ground on which you stand, and sing to you
as they spread out their wings to keep you safe,
and shelter you from every worldly thought
that would intrude upon your holiness.

Repeat the Name of God, and call upon
your Self, Whose Name is His. Repeat His Name,
and all the tiny, nameless things on earth
slip into right perspective. Those who call
upon the Name of God can not mistake
the nameless for the Name, nor sin for grace,
nor bodies for the holy Son of God.
And should you join a brother as you sit
with him in silence, and repeat God's Name
along with him within your quiet mind,
you have established there an altar which
reaches to God Himself and to His Son.

Turn to the Name of God for your release,
and it is given you. No prayer but this
is necessary, for it holds them all
within it. Words are insignificant,
and all requests unneeded when God's Son
calls on his Father's Name. His Father's Thoughts
become his own. He makes his claim to all
his Father gave, is giving still, and will
forever give. He calls on Him to let
all things he thought he made be nameless now,
and in their place the holy Name of God
becomes his judgment of their worthlessness.

All little things are silent. Little sounds
are soundless now. The little things of earth
have disappeared. The universe consists
of nothing but the Son of God, who calls
upon his Father. And his Father's Voice
gives answer in his Father's holy Name.
In this eternal, still relationship,
in which communication far transcends
all words, and yet exceeds in depth and height
whatever words could possibly convey,
is peace eternal. In our Father's Name,
we would experience this peace today.
And in His Name, it shall be given us.

i **rest in God.** Completely undismayed,
this thought will carry you through storms and strife,
past misery and pain, past loss and death,
and onward to the certainty of God.
There is no suffering it cannot heal.
There is no problem that it cannot solve.
And no appearance but will turn to truth
before the eyes of you who rest in God.

You rest within the peace of God today,
and call upon your brothers from your rest
to draw them to their rest, along with you.
You will be faithful to your trust today,
forgetting no one, bringing everyone
into the boundless circle of your peace,
the holy sanctuary where you rest.
Open the temple doors and let them come
from far across the world, and near as well;
your distant brothers and your closest friends;
bid them all enter here and rest with you.

*g*od speaks to us. Shall we not speak to Him?
He is not distant. He makes no attempt
to hide from us. We try to hide from Him,
and suffer from deception. He remains
entirely accessible. He loves
His Son. There is no certainty but this,
yet this suffices. He will love His Son
forever. When his mind remains asleep,
He loves him still. And when his mind awakes,
He loves him with a never-changing Love.

If you but knew the meaning of His Love,
hope and despair would be impossible.
For hope would be forever satisfied;
despair of any kind unthinkable.
His grace His answer is to all despair,
for in it lies remembrance of His Love.
Would He not gladly give the means by which
His Will is recognized? His grace is yours
by your acknowledgment. And memory
of Him awakens in the mind that asks
the means of Him whereby its sleep is done.

Your grace is given me. I claim it now.
Father, I come to You. And You will come
to me who ask. I am the Son You love.

Father, Your holiness is mine. Your Love
created me, and made my sinlessness
forever part of You. I have no guilt
nor sin in me, for there is none in You.

there is a place in you where this whole world
has been forgotten; where no memory
of sin and of illusion linger still.
There is a place in you which time has left,
and echoes of eternity are heard.
There is a resting place so still no sound
except a hymn to Heaven rises up
to gladden God the Father and the Son.
Where both abide are They remembered, both.
And where They are is Heaven and is peace.

Think not that you can change Their dwelling place.
For your Identity abides in Them,
and where They are, forever must you be.
The changelessness of Heaven is in you,
so deep within that nothing in this world
but passes by, unnoticed and unseen.
The still infinity of endless peace
surrounds you gently in its soft embrace,
so strong and quiet, tranquil in the might
of its Creator, nothing can intrude
upon the sacred Son of God within.

*W*hat can correct illusions but the truth?
And what are errors but illusions that
remain unrecognized for what they are?
Where truth has entered errors disappear.
They merely vanish, leaving not a trace
by which to be remembered. They are gone
because, without belief, they have no life,
And so they disappear to nothingness,
returning whence they came. From dust to dust
they come and go, for only truth remains.

Truth does not come and go nor shift nor change,
in this appearance now and then in that,
evading capture and escaping grasp.
It does not hide. It stands in open light,
in obvious accessibility.
It is impossible that anyone
could seek it truly, and would not succeed.
Today belongs to truth. Give truth its due,
and it will give you yours. You were not meant
to suffer and to die. Your Father wills
these dreams be gone. Let truth correct them all.

Truth will correct all errors in my mind,
and I will rest in Him Who is my Self.

there are not different kinds of life, for life
is like the truth. It does not have degrees.
It is the one condition in which all
that God created share. Like all His Thoughts,
it has no opposite. There is no death
because what God created shares His Life.
There is no death because an opposite
to God does not exist. There is no death
because the Father and the Son are one.

The mind can think it sleeps, but that is all.
It cannot change what is its waking state.
It cannot make a body, nor abide
within a body. What is alien to
the mind does not exist, because it has
no source. For mind creates all things that are,
and cannot give them attributes it
lacks, nor change its own eternal, mindful state.
It cannot make the physical. What seems
to die is but the sign of mind asleep.

God creates only mind awake. He does
not sleep, and His creations cannot share
what He gives not, nor make conditions which
He does not share with them. The thought of death
is not the opposite to thoughts of life.
Forever unopposed by opposites
of any kind, the Thoughts of God remain
forever changeless, with the power to
extend forever changelessly, but yet
within themselves, for they are everywhere.

What seems to be the opposite of life
is merely sleeping. When the mind elects
to be what it is not, and to assume an
alien power which it does not have, a
foreign state it cannot enter, or a
false condition not within its Source, it
merely seems to go to sleep a while. It
dreams of time; an interval in which what
seems to happen never has occurred,
the changes wrought are substanceless, and all
events are nowhere. When the mind awakes,
it but continues as it always was.

We share our life because we have one Source,
a Source from Which perfection comes to us,
remaining always in the holy minds
which He created perfect. As we were,
so are we now and will forever be
A sleeping mind must waken, as it sees
its own perfection mirroring the Lord
of Life so perfectly it fades into
what is reflected there. And now it is
no more a mere reflection. It becomes
the thing reflected, and the light which makes
reflection possible. No vision now
is needed. For the wakened mind is one
that knows its Source, its Self, its Holiness.

*M*y true Identity is so secure,
so lofty, sinless, glorious and great,
wholly beneficent and free from guilt,
that Heaven looks to It to give it light.
It lights the world as well. It is the gift
my Father gave to me; the one as well
I give the world. There is no gift but This
that can be either given or received.
This is reality, and only This.
This is illusion's end. It is the truth.

My Name, O Father, still is known to You.
I have forgotten it, and do not know
where I am going, who I am, or what
it is I do. Remind me, Father, now,
for I am weary of the world I see.
Reveal what You would have me see instead.

the world you see holds nothing that you need
to offer you; nothing that you can use
in any way, nor anything at all
that serves to give you joy. Believe this thought,
and you are saved from years of misery,
from countless disappointments, and from hopes
that turn to bitter ashes of despair.
No one but must accept this thought as true,
if he would leave the world behind and soar
beyond its petty scope and little ways.

Each thing you value here is but a chain
that binds you to the world, and it will serve
no other end but this. For everything
must serve the purpose you have given it,
until you see a different purpose there.
The only purpose worthy of your mind
this world contains is that you pass it by,
without delaying to perceive some hope
where there is none. Be you deceived no more.
The world you see holds nothing that you want.

Peace and be still a little while, and see
how far you rise above the world, when you
release your mind from chains and let it seek
the level where it finds itself at home.
It will be grateful to be free a while.
It knows where it belongs. But free its wings,
and it will fly in sureness and in joy
to join its holy purpose. Let it rest
in its Creator, there to be restored
to sanity, to freedom and to love.

*n*o one can give what he has not received.
To give a thing requires first you have
it in your own possession. Here the laws
of Heaven and the world agree. But here
they also separate. The world believes
that to possess a thing, it must be kept.
Salvation teaches otherwise. To give
is how to recognize you have received.
It is the proof that what you have is yours.

You understand that you are healed when you
give healing. You accept forgiveness as
accomplished in yourself when you forgive.
You recognize your brother as yourself,
and thus do you perceive that you are whole.
There is no miracle you cannot give,
for all are given you. Receive them now
by opening the storehouse of your mind
where they are laid, and giving them away.

*t**here** is no gift the Father asks of you
but that you see in all creation but
the shining glory of His gift to you.
Behold His Son, His perfect gift, in whom
his Father shines forever, and to whom
is all creation given as his own.
Because he has it is it given you,
and where it lies in him behold your peace.
The quiet that surrounds you dwells in him,
and from this quiet come the happy dreams
in which your hands are joined in innocence.
These are not hands that grasp in dreams of pain.
They hold no sword, for they have left their hold
on every vain illusion of this world.
And being empty they receive, instead,
a brother's hand in which completion lies.

the Thoughts of God are far beyond all change,
and shine forever. They await not birth.
They wait for welcome and remembering.
The Thought God holds of you is like a star,
unchangeable in an eternal sky.
So high in Heaven is it set that those
outside of Heaven know not it is there.
Yet still and white and lovely will it shine
through all eternity. There was no time
it was not there; no instant when its lights
grew dimmer or less perfect ever was.

Who knows the Father knows this light, for He
is the eternal sky that holds it safe,
forever lifted up and anchored sure.
Its perfect purity does not depend
on whether it is seen on earth or not.
The sky embraces it and softly holds
it in its perfect place, which is as far
from earth as earth from Heaven. It is not
the distance nor the time that keeps this star
invisible to earth. But those who seek
for idols cannot know the star is there.

Beyond all idols is the Thought God holds
of you. Completely unaffected by
the turmoil and the terror of the world,
the dreams of birth and death that here are dreamed,
the myriad of forms that fear can take;
quite undisturbed, the Thought God holds of you
remains exactly as it always was.
Surrounded by a stillness so complete
no sound of battle comes remotely near;
it rests in certainty and perfect peace.

Here is your one reality kept safe,
completely unaware of all the world
that worships idols, and that knows not God.
In perfect sureness of its changelessness
and of its rest in its eternal home,
the Thought God holds of you has never left
the Mind of its Creator, Whom it knows
as its Creator knows that it is there.

Where could the Thought God holds of you exist
but where you are? Is your reality
a thing apart from you, and in a world
which your reality knows nothing of?
Outside you there is no eternal sky,
no changeless star and no reality.
The mind of Heaven's Son in Heaven is,
for there the Mind of Father and of Son
joined in creation which can have no end.
You have not two realities, but one.
Nor can you be aware of more than one.
An idol *or* the Thought God holds of you
is your reality. Forget not, then,
that idols must keep hidden what you are,
not from the Mind of God, but from your own.
The star shines still; the sky has never changed.
But you, the holy Son of God Himself,
are unaware of your reality.

father, You stand before me and behind,
beside me, in the place I see myself,
and everywhere I go. You are in all
the things I look upon, the sounds I hear,
and every hand that reaches for my own.
In You time disappears, and place becomes
a meaningless belief. For what surrounds
Your Son and keeps him safe is Love Itself.
There is no Source but This, and nothing is
that does not share Its holiness; that stands
beyond Your one creation, or without
the Love Which holds all things within Itself.
Father, Your Son is like Yourself. We come
to You in Your Own Name today, to be
at peace within Your everlasting Love.

i am the Son of God. No body can
contain my spirit, nor impose on me
a limitation God created not.

i was mistaken when I thought I lived
apart from God, a separate entity
that moved in isolation, unattached,
and housed within a body. Now I know
my life is God's, I have no other home,
and I do not exist apart from Him.
He has no Thoughts that are not part of me,
and I have none but those which are of Him.

*i*f I accept that I am prisoner
within a body, in a world in which
all things that seem to live appear to die,
then is my Father prisoner with me.
And this do I believe, when I maintain
the laws the world obeys must I obey;
the frailties and the sins which I perceive
are real, and cannot be escaped. If I
am bound in any way, I do not know
my Father nor my Self. And I am lost
to all reality. For truth is free,
and what is bound is not a part of truth.

father, I was mistaken in myself,
because I failed to realize the Source
from Which I came. I have not left that Source
to enter in a body and to die.
My holiness remains a part of me,
as I am part of You. And my mistakes
about myself are dreams. I let them go
today. And I stand ready to receive
Your Word alone for what I really am.

this is God's Final Judgment: "You are still
My holy Son, forever innocent,
forever loving and forever loved,
as limitless as your Creator, and
completely changeless and forever pure.
Therefore awaken and return to Me.
I am Your Father and you are My Son."

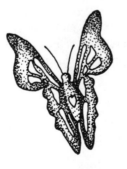

Love is my heritage, and with it joy.
These are the gifts my Father gave to me.
I would accept all that is mine in truth.

*P*erhaps you think that different kinds of love
are possible. Perhaps you think there is
a kind of love for this, a kind for that;
a way of loving one, another way
of loving still another. Love is one.
It has no separate parts and no degrees;
no kinds nor levels, no divergencies
and no distinctions. It is like itself,
unchanged throughout. It never alters with
a person or a circumstance. It is
the Heart of God, and also of His Son.

Love cannot judge. As it is one itself,
it looks on all as one. Its meaning lies
in oneness. And it must elude the mind
that thinks of it as partial or in part.
There is no love but God's, and all of love
is His. There is no other principle
that rules where love is not. Love is a law
without an opposite. Its wholeness is
the power holding everything as one,
the link between the Father and the Son
which holds them both forever as the same.

I bless you, brother, with the Love of God,
which I would share with you. For I would learn
the joyous lesson that there is no love
but God's and yours and mine and everyone's.

*h*appiness is an attribute of love.
It cannot be apart from it. Nor can
it be experienced where love is not.
Love has no limits, being everywhere.
And therefore joy is everywhere as well.
Yet can the mind deny that this is so,
believing there are gaps in love where sin
can enter, bringing pain instead of joy.
This strange belief would limit happiness
by redefining love as limited,
and introducing opposition in
what has no limit and no opposite.

God, being Love, is also happiness.
To fear Him is to be afraid of joy.

*f*ather, I must return Your Love for me,
for giving and receiving are the same,
and You have given all Your Love to me.
I must return it, for I want it mine
in full awareness, blazing in my mind
and keeping it within its kindly light,
inviolate, beloved, with fear behind
and only peace ahead. How still the way
Your loving Son is led along to You!

Surrounding me is all the life that God
created in His Love. It calls to me
in every heartbeat and in every breath;
in every action and in every thought.
Peace fills my heart, and floods my body with
the purpose of forgiveness. Now my mind
is healed, and all I need to save the world
is given me. Each heartbeat brings me peace;
each breath infuses me with strength. I am
a messenger of God, directed by
His Voice, sustained by Him in love, and held
forever quiet and at peace within
His loving Arms. Each heartbeat calls His Name,
and every one is answered by His Voice,
assuring me I am at home in Him.

Let me attend Your Answer, not my own.
Father, my heart is beating in the peace
the Heart of Love created. It is there
and only there that I can be at home.

Creation is the sum of all God's Thoughts
in number infinite, and everywhere
without all limit. Only Love creates,
and only like Itself. There was no time
when all that It created was not there.
Nor will there be a time when anything
that It created suffers any loss.
Forever and forever are God's Thoughts
exactly as they were and as they are,
unchanged through time and after time is done.

We are creation; we the Sons of God.
We seem to be discrete, and unaware
of our eternal unity with Him.
Yet back of all our doubts, past all our fears,
there still is certainty. For Love remains
with all Its Thoughts, Its sureness being theirs.
God's memory is in our holy minds,
which know their oneness and their unity
with their Creator. Let our function be
only to let this memory return,
only to let God's Will be done on earth,
only to be restored to sanity,
and to be but as God created us.

i feel the Love of God within me now.

There is a light in you the world can not
perceive. And with its eyes you will not see
this light, for you are blinded by the world.
Yet you have eyes to see it. It is there
for you to look upon. It was not placed
in you to be kept hidden from your sight.
This light is a reflection of the thought
we practice now. To feel the Love of God
within you is to see the world anew,
shining in innocence, alive with hope,
and blessed with perfect charity and love.

Who could feel fear in such a world as this?
It welcomes you, rejoices that you came,
and sings your praises as it keeps you safe
from every form of danger and of pain.
It offers you a warm and gentle home
in which to stay a while. It blesses you
throughout the day, and watches through the night
as silent guardian of your holy sleep.
It sees salvation in you, and protects
the light in you, in which it sees its own.
It offers you its flowers and its snow,
in thankfulness for your benevolence.
This is the world the Love of God reveals.

Father, we do not know the way to You.
But we have called, and You have answered us.
We will not interfere. Salvation's ways
are not our own, for they belong to You.
And it is unto You we look for them.
Our hands are open to receive Your gifts.
We have no thoughts we think apart from You,
and cherish no beliefs of what we are,
or Who created us. Yours is the way
that we would find and follow. And we ask
but that Your Will, which is our own as well,
be done in us and in the world, that it
become a part of Heaven now. Amen.

Father, I come to You today to seek
the peace that You alone can give. I
come in silence. In the quiet of my heart,
the deep recesses of my mind, I wait and
listen for Your Voice. My Father, speak
to me today. I come to hear Your Voice
in silence and in certainty and love, sure
You will hear my call and answer me.

*f*ather, I wake today with miracles
correcting my perception of all things.
And so begins the day I share with You
as I will share eternity, for time
has stepped aside today. I do not seek
the things of time, and so I will not look
upon them. What I seek today transcends
all laws of time and things perceived in time.
I would forget all things except Your Love.
I would abide in You, and know no laws
except Your law of love. And I would find
the peace which You created for Your Son,
forgetting all the foolish toys I made
as I behold Your glory and my own.

*U*nless the past is over in my mind,
the real world must escape my sight. For I
am really looking nowhere; seeing but
what is not there. How can I then perceive
the world forgiveness offers? This the past
was made to hide, for this the world that can
be looked on only now. It has no past.
For what can be forgiven but the past,
and if it is forgiven it is gone.

*g*od holds your future as He holds your past
and present. They are one to Him, and so
they should be one to you. Yet in this world,
the temporal progression still seems real.
And so you are not asked to understand
the lack of sequence really found in time.
You are but asked to let the future go,
and place it in God's Hands. And you will see
by your experience that you have laid
the past and present in His Hands as well,
because the past will punish you no more,
and future dread will now be meaningless.

Release the future. For the past is gone,
and what is present, freed from its bequest
of grief and misery, of pain and loss,
becomes the instant in which time escapes
the bondage of illusions where it runs
its pitiless, inevitable course.
Then is each instant which was slave to time
transformed into a holy instant, when
the light that was kept hidden in God's Son
is freed to bless the world. Now is he free,
and all his glory shines upon a world
made free with him, to share his holiness.

Place, then, your future in the Hands of God.
For thus you call the memory of Him
to come again, replacing all your thoughts
of sin and evil with the truth of love.
Think you the world could fail to gain thereby,
and every living creature not respond
with healed perception? Who entrusts himself
to God has also placed the world within
the Hands to which he has himself appealed
for comfort and security. He lays
aside the sick illusions of the world
along with his, and offers peace to both.

Now are we saved indeed. For in God's Hands
we rest untroubled, sure that only good
can come to us. If we forget, we will
be gently reassured. If we accept
an unforgiving thought, it will be soon
replaced by love's reflection. And if we
are tempted to attack, we will appeal
to Him Who guards our rest to make the choice
for us that leaves temptation far behind.
No longer is the world our enemy,
for we have chosen that we be its Friend.

The peace of God is everything I want.
The peace of God is my one goal; the aim
of all my living here, the end I seek,
my purpose and my function and my life,
while I abide where I am not at home.

*W*hy wait for Heaven? Those who seek the light
are merely covering their eyes. The light
is in them now. Enlightenment is but
a recognition, not a change at all.
Light is not of the world, yet you who bear
the light in you are alien here as well.
The light came with you from your native home,
and stayed with you because it is your own.
It is the only thing you bring with you
from Him Who is your Source. It shines in you
because it lights your home, and leads you back
to where it came from and you are at home.

This light can not be lost. Why wait to find
it in the future, or believe it has
been lost already, or was never there?
It can so easily be looked upon
that arguments which prove it is not there
become ridiculous. Who can deny
the presence of what he beholds in him?
It is not difficult to look within,
for there all vision starts. There is no sight,
be it of dreams or from a truer Source,
that is not but the shadow of the seen
through inward vision. There perception starts,
and there it ends. It has no source but this.

The peace of God is shining in you now,
and from your heart extends around the world.
It pauses to caress each living thing,
and leaves a blessing with it that remains
forever and forever. What it gives
must be eternal. It removes all thoughts
of the ephemeral and valueless.
It brings renewal to all tired hearts,
and lights all vision as it passes by.
All of its gifts are given everyone,
and everyone unites in giving thanks
to you who give, and you who have received.

The shining in your mind reminds the world
of what it has forgotten, and the world
restores the memory to you as well.
From you salvation radiates with gifts
beyond all measure, given and returned.
To you, the giver of the gift, does God
Himself give thanks. And in His blessing does
the light in you shine brighter, adding to
the gifts you have to offer to the world.

The peace of God is shining in me now.
Let all things shine upon me in that peace,
and let me bless them with the light in me.

*i*n peace I was created. And in peace
do I remain. It is not given me
to change my Self. How merciful is God
my Father, that when He created me
He gave me peace forever. Now I ask
but to be what I am. And can this be
denied me, when it is forever true?

Father, I seek the peace you gave as mine
in my creation. What was given then
must be here now, for my creation was
apart from time, and still remains beyond
all change. The peace in which Your Son was born
into Your Mind is shining there unchanged.
I am as You created me. I need
but call on You to find the peace You gave.
It is Your Will that gave it to Your Son.

Your peace surrounds me, Father. Where I go,
Your peace goes there with me. It sheds its light
on everyone I meet. I bring it to
the desolate and lonely and afraid.
I give Your peace to those who suffer pain,
or grieve for loss, or think they are bereft
of hope and happiness. Send them to me,
my Father. Let me bring Your peace with me.
For I would save Your Son, as is Your Will,
that I may come to recognize my Self.

*i*t does not seem to me that I can choose
to have but peace today. And yet, my God
assures me that His Son is like Himself.
Let me this day have faith in Him Who says
I am God's Son. And let the peace I choose
be mine today bear witness to the truth
of what He says. God's Son can have no cares,
and must remain forever in the peace
of Heaven. In His name, I give today
to finding what my Father wills for me,
accepting it as mine, and giving it
to all my Father's Sons, along with me.

*t*oday we would remove all meaningless
and self-made gifts which we have placed upon
the holy altar where God's gifts belong.
His are the gifts that are our own in truth.
His are the gifts that we inherited
before time was, and that will still be ours
when time has passed into eternity.
His are the gifts that are within us now,
for they are timeless. And we need not wait
to have them. They belong to us today.

Therefore, we choose to have them now, and know,
in choosing them in place of what we made,
we but unite our will with what God wills,
and recognize the same as being one.

I seek but what belongs to me in truth,
and joy and peace are my inheritance.

I seek but what belongs to me in truth.
God's gifts of joy and peace are all I want.

i am the home of light and joy and peace.
I welcome them into the home I share
with God, because I am a part of Him.

*t*oday I will accept God's peace and joy,
in glad exchange for all the substitutes
that I have made for happiness and peace.

abide in peace, where God would have you be.
And be the means whereby your brother finds
the peace in which your wishes are fulfilled.
Let us unite in bringing blessing to
the world of sin and death. For what can save
each one of us can save us all. There is
no difference among the Sons of God.
The unity that specialness denies
will save them all, for what is one can have
no specialness. And everything belongs
to each of them. No wishes lie between
a brother and his own. To get from one
is to deprive them all. And yet to bless
but one gives blessing to them all as one.

*a*s Heaven's peace and joy intensify
when you accept them as God's gift to you,
so does the joy of your Creator grow
when you accept His joy and peace as yours.
True giving is creation. It extends
the limitless to the unlimited,
eternity to timelessness, and love
unto itself. It adds to all that is
complete already, not in simple terms
of adding more, for that implies that it
was less before. It adds by letting what
cannot contain itself fulfill its aim
of giving everything it has away,
securing it forever for itself.

My brother, peace and joy I offer you,
that I may have God's peace and joy as mine.

father, let me remember You are here,
and I am not alone. Surrounding me
is everlasting Love. I have no cause
for anything except the perfect peace
and joy I share with You. What need have I
for anger or for fear? Surrounding me
is perfect safety. Can I be afraid,
when Your eternal promise goes with me?
Surrounding me is perfect sinlessness.
What can I fear, when You created me
in holiness as perfect as Your Own?

i want the peace of God . . .

To say these words is nothing. But to mean
these words is everything. If you could but
mean them for just an instant, there would be
no further sorrow possible for you
in any form; in any place or time.
Heaven would be completely given back
to full awareness, memory of God
entirely restored, the resurrection
of all creation fully recognized.

No one can mean these words and not be healed.
He cannot play with dreams, nor think he is
himself a dream. He cannot make a hell
and think it real. He wants the peace of God,
and it is given him. For that is all
he wants, and that is all he will receive.
Many have said these words. But few indeed
have meant them. You have but to look upon
the world you see around you to be sure
how very few they are. The world would
be completely changed, should any two agree
these words express the only thing they want.

The mind which means that all it wants is peace
must join with other minds, for that is how
peace is obtained. And when the wish for peace
is genuine, the means for finding it
is given, in a form each mind that seeks
for it in honesty can understand.
Whatever form the lesson takes is planned
for him in such a way that he can not
mistake it, if his asking is sincere.
But if he asks without sincerity,
there is no form in which the lesson will
meet with acceptance and be truly learned.

No one who truly seeks the peace of God
can fail to find it. For he merely asks
that he deceive himself no longer by
denying to himself what is God's Will.
Who can remain unsatisfied who asks
for what he has already? Who could be
unanswered who requests an answer which
is his to give? The peace of God is yours.

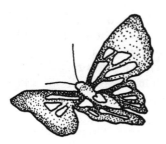

What can my function be but to accept the Word of God, Who has created me for what I am and will forever be?

*S*alvation *of the world depends on me.*

Here is the statement that will one day take
all arrogance away from every mind.
Here is the thought of true humility,
which holds no function as your own but that
which has been given you. It offers your
acceptance of a part assigned to you,
without insisting on another role.
It does not judge your proper role. It but
acknowledges the Will of God is done
on earth as well as Heaven. It unites
all wills on earth in Heaven's plan to save
the world, restoring it to Heaven's peace.

There is one way, and only one, to be
released from the imprisonment your plan
to prove the false is true has brought to you.
Accept the plan you did not make instead.
Judge not your value to it. If God's Voice
assures you that salvation needs your part,
and that the whole depends on you, be sure
that it is so. The arrogant must cling
to words, afraid to go beyond them to
experience which might affront their stance.
Yet are the humble free to hear the Voice
Which tells them what they are, and what to do.

each day a thousand treasures come to me
with every passing moment. I am blessed
with gifts throughout the day, in value far
beyond all things of which I can conceive.
A brother smiles upon another, and
my heart is gladdened. Someone speaks a word
of gratitude or mercy, and my mind
receives this gift and takes it as its own.
And everyone who finds the way to God
becomes my savior, pointing out the way
to me, and giving me his certainty
that what he learned is surely mine as well.

*S*alvation is a promise, made by God,
that you would find your way to Him at last.
It cannot but be kept. It guarantees
that time will have an end, and all the thoughts
that have been born in time will end as well.
God's Word is given every mind which thinks
that it has separate thoughts, and will replace
these thoughts of conflict with the Thought of peace.

Salvation is undoing in the sense
that it does nothing, failing to support
the world of dreams and malice. Thus it lets
illusions go. By not supporting them,
it merely lets them quietly go down
to dust. And what they hid is now revealed;
an altar to the holy Name of God
whereon His Word is written, with the gifts
of your forgiveness laid before it, and
the memory of God not far behind.

*t*his is salvation's keynote: What I see
reflects a process in my mind, which starts
with my idea of what I want. From there,
the mind makes up an image of the thing
the mind desires, judges valuable,
and therefore seeks to find. These images
are then projected outward, looked upon,
esteemed as real and guarded as one's own.
From insane wishes comes an insane world.
From judgment comes a world condemned. And from
forgiving thoughts a gentle world comes forth,
with mercy for the holy Son of God,
to offer him a kindly home where he
can rest a while before he journeys on,
and help his brothers walk ahead with him,
and find the way to Heaven and to God.

*t**he** concept of yourself that now you hold
would guarantee your function here remain
forever unaccomplished and undone.
And thus it dooms you to a bitter sense
of deep depression and futility.
Yet it need not be fixed, unless you choose
to hold it past the hope of change and keep
it static and concealed within your mind.
Give it instead to Him Who understands
the changes that it needs to let it serve
the function given you to bring you peace,
that you may offer peace to have it yours.
Alternatives are in your mind to use,
and you can see yourself another way.
Would you not rather look upon yourself
as needed for salvation of the world,
instead of as salvation's enemy?

The concept of the self stands like a shield,
a silent barricade before the truth,
and hides it from your sight. All things you see
are images, because you look on them
as through a barrier that dims your sight
and warps your vision, so that you behold
nothing with clarity. The light is kept
from everything you see. At most, you glimpse
a shadow of what lies beyond. At least,
you merely look on darkness, and perceive
the terrified imaginings that come
from guilty thoughts and concepts born of fear.
And what you see is hell, for fear *is* hell.
All that is given you is for release;
the sight, the vision and the inner Guide
all lead you out of hell with those you love
beside you, and the universe with them.

Behold your role within the universe!
To every part of true creation has
the Lord of Love and Life entrusted all
salvation from the misery of hell.
And to each one has He allowed the grace
to be a savior to the holy ones
especially entrusted to his care.
And this he learns when first he looks upon
one brother as he looks upon himself,
and sees the mirror of himself in him.
Thus is the concept of himself laid by,
for nothing stands between his sight and what
he looks upon, to judge what he beholds.
And in this single vision does he see
the face of Christ, and understands he looks
on everyone as he beholds this one.
For there is light where darkness was before,
and now the veil is lifted from his sight.

all that is needful is to train our minds
to overlook all little senseless aims,
and to remember that our goal is God.
His memory is hidden in our minds,
obscured but by our pointless little goals
which offer nothing, and do not exist.
Shall we continue to allow God's grace
to shine in unawareness, while the toys
and trinkets of the world are sought instead?
God is our only goal, our only Love.
We have no aim but to remember Him.

today I will accept the truth about
myself. I will arise in glory, and
allow the light in me to shine upon
the world throughout the day. I bring the world
the tidings of salvation which I hear
as God my Father speaks to me. And I
behold the world that Christ would have me see,
aware it ends the bitter dream of death;
aware it is my Father's call to me.

I share my Father's Will for me, His Son.
What He has given me is all I want.
What He has given me is all there is.
I share God's Will for happiness for me.

*f*ather, Your Will is mine, and only that.
There is no other will for me to have.
Let me not try to make another will,
for it is senseless and will cause me pain.
Your Will alone can bring me happiness,
and only Yours exists. If I would have
what only You can give, I must accept
Your Will for me, and enter into peace
where conflict is impossible, Your Son
is one with You in being and in will,
and nothing contradicts the holy truth
that I remain as You created me.

i have a kingdom I must rule. At times,
it does not seem I am its king at all.
It seems to triumph over me, and tell
me what to think, and what to do and feel.
And yet it has been given me to serve
whatever purpose I perceive in it.
My mind can only serve. Today I give
its service to the Holy Spirit to
employ as He sees fit. I thus direct
my mind, which I alone can rule. And thus
I set it free to do the Will of God.

father, I give You all my thoughts today.
I would have none of mine. In place of them,
give me Your Own. I give You all my acts
as well, that I may do Your Will instead
of seeking goals which cannot be obtained,
and wasting time in vain imaginings.
Today I come to You. I will step back
and merely follow You. Be You the Guide,
and I the follower who questions not
the wisdom of the Infinite, nor Love
whose tenderness I cannot conprehend,
but which is yet Your perfect gift to me.

i need but look upon all things that seem
to hurt me, and with perfect certainty
assure myself, "God wills that I be saved
from this," and merely watch them disappear.
I need but keep in mind my Father's Will
for me is only happiness, to find
that only happiness has come to me.
And I need but remember that God's Love
surrounds His Son and keeps his sinlessness
forever perfect, to be sure that I
am saved and safe forever in His Arms.
I am the Son He loves. And I am saved
because God in His mercy wills it so.

father, it is today that I am free,
because my will is Yours. I thought to make
another will. Yet nothing that I thought
apart from You exists. And I am free
because I was mistaken, and did not
affect my own reality at all
by my illusions. Now I give them up,
and lay them down before the feet of truth,
to be removed forever from my mind.
This is my holy instant of release.
Father, I know my will is one with Yours.

*n*o one can lose and everyone must gain
whenever any gift of God has been
requested and received by anyone.
God gives but to unite. To take away
is meaningless to Him. And when it is
as meaningless to you, you can be sure
you share one Will with Him, and He with you.
And you will also know you share one Will
with all your brothers, whose intent is yours.

*g*od's Will is perfect happiness for me.
And I can suffer but from the belief
there is another will apart from His.

I will forgive all things today, that I may learn how to accept the truth in me, and come to recognize my sinlessness.

*f*orgiveness recognizes what you thought
your brother did to you has not occurred.
It does not pardon sins and make them real.
It sees there was no sin. And in that view
are all your sins forgiven. What is sin,
except a false idea about God's Son?
Forgiveness merely sees its falsity,
and therefore lets it go. What then is free
to take its place is now the Will of God.

An unforgiving thought does many things.
In frantic action it pursues its goal,
twisting and overturning what it sees
as interfering with its chosen path.
Distortion is its purpose, and the means
by which it would accomplish it as well.
It sets about its furious attempts
to smash reality, without concern
for anything that would appear to pose
a contradiction to its point of view.

Forgiveness, on the other hand, is still
and quietly does nothing. It offends
no aspect of reality, nor seeks
to twist it to appearances it likes.
It merely looks, and waits, and judges not.
He who would not forgive must judge, for he
must justify his failure to forgive.
But he who would forgive himself must learn
to welcome truth exactly as it is.

Do nothing, then, and let forgiveness show
you what to do, through Him Who is your Guide,
your Savior and Protector, strong in hope,
and certain of your ultimate success.
He has forgiven you already, for
such is His function, given Him by God.
Now must you share His function, and forgive
whom He has saved, whose sinlessness He sees,
and whom He honors as the Son of God.

*f*orgiveness is the only gift I give,
because it is the only gift I want.
And everything I give I give myself.
This is salvation's simple formula.
And I, who would be saved, would make it mine,
to be the way I live within a world
that needs salvation, and that will be saved
as I accept Atonement for myself.

*f*ather, unless I judge I cannot weep.
Nor can I suffer pain, or feel I am
abandoned or unneeded in the world.
This is my home because I judge it not,
and therefore is it only what You will.
Let me today behold it uncondemned,
through happy eyes forgiveness has released
from all distortion. Let me see Your world
instead of mine. And all the tears I shed
will be forgotten, for their source is gone.
Father, I will not judge Your world today.

*f*orgiveness, truth's reflection, tells me how
to offer miracles, and thus escape
the prison house in which I think I live.
Your holy Son is pointed out to me,
first in my brother; then in me. Your Voice
instructs me patiently to hear Your Word,
and give as I receive. And as I look
upon Your Son today, I hear Your Voice
instructing me to find the way to You,
as You appointed that the way shall be:
"Behold his sinlessness, and be you healed."

*f*orgiveness is the key to happiness.
I will awaken from the dream that I
am mortal, fallible and full of sin,
and know I am the perfect Son of God.

*f*orgiveness gently looks upon all things
unknown in Heaven, sees them disappear,
and leaves the world a clean and unmarked slate
on which the Word of God can now replace
the senseless symbols written there before.
Forgiveness is the means by which the fear
of death is overcome, because it holds
no fierce attraction now and guilt is gone.
Forgiveness lets the body be perceived
as what it is; a simple teaching aid,
to be laid by when learning is complete,
but hardly changing him who learns at all.

The mind without the body cannot make
mistakes. It cannot think that it will die,
nor be the prey of merciless attack.
Anger becomes impossible, and where
is terror then? What fears could still assail
those who have lost the source of all attack,
the core of anguish and the seat of fear?
Only forgiveness can relieve the mind
of thinking that the body is its home.
Only forgiveness can restore the peace
that God intended for His holy Son.
Only forgiveness can persuade the Son
to look again upon his holiness.

What could you want forgiveness cannot give?
Do you want peace? Forgiveness offers it.
Do you want happiness, a quiet mind,
a certainty of purpose, and a sense
of worth and beauty that transcends the world?
Do you want care and safety, and the warmth
of sure protection always? Do you want
a quietness that cannot be disturbed,
a gentleness that never can be hurt,
a deep, abiding comfort, and a rest
so perfect it can never be upset?

Here is the answer! Would you stand outside
while all of Heaven waits for you within?
Forgive and be forgiven. As you give
you will receive. There is no plan but this
for the salvation of the Son of God.
Let us today rejoice that this is so,
for here we have an answer, clear and plain,
beyond deceit in its simplicity.
All the complexities the world has spun
of fragile cobwebs disappear before
the power and the majesty of this
extremely simple statement of the truth.

Forgiveness offers everything I want.
Today I have accepted this as true.
Today I have received the gifts of God.

*f*orgiveness paints a picture of a world
where suffering is over, loss becomes
impossible and anger makes no sense.
Attack is gone, and madness has an end.
What suffering is now conceivable?
What loss can be sustained? The world becomes
a place of joy, abundance, charity
and endless giving. It is now so like
to Heaven that it quickly is transformed
into the light that it reflects. And so
the journey which the Son of God began
has ended in the light from which he came.

all things are lessons God would have you learn.
He would not leave an unforgiving thought
without correction, nor one thorn or nail
to hurt His holy Son in any way.
He would ensure his holy rest remain
untroubled and serene, without a care,
in an eternal home which cares for him.
And He would have all tears be wiped away,
with none remaining yet unshed, and none
but waiting their appointed time to fall.
For God has willed that laughter should replace
each one, and that His Son be free again.

This is the lesson God would have you learn:
There is a way to look on everything
that lets it be to you another step
to Him, and to salvation of the world.
To all that speaks of terror, answer thus:
"I will forgive, and this will disappear."
To every apprehension, every care
and every form of suffering, repeat
these selfsame words. And then you hold the key
that opens Heaven's gate, and brings the Love
of God the Father down to earth at last,
to raise it up to Heaven. God will take
this final step Himself. Do not deny
the little steps He asks you take to Him.

I am God's Son. Today I lay aside all sick illusions of myself, and let my Father, tell me Who I really am.

father, I was created in Your Mind,
a holy Thought that never left its home.
I am forever Your Effect, and You
forever and forever are my Cause.
As You created me I have remained.
Where You established me I still abide.
And all Your attributes abide in me,
because it is Your Will to have a Son
so like his Cause that Cause and its Effect
are indistinguishable. Let me know
that I am an Effect of God, and so
I have the power to create like You.
And as it is in Heaven, so on earth.
Your plan I follow here, and at the end
I know that You will gather Your effects
into the tranquil Heaven of Your Love,
where earth will vanish, and all separate thoughts
unite in glory as the Son of God.

*t*he end of suffering can not be loss.
The gift of everything can be but gain.
You only give. You never take away.
And You created me to be like You,
so sacrifice becomes impossible
for me as well as You. I, too, must give.
And so all things are given unto me
forever and forever. As I was
created I remain. Your Son can make
no sacrifice, for he must be complete,
having the function of completing You.
I am complete because I am Your Son.
I cannot lose, for I can only give,
and everything is mine eternally.

i am God's Son, complete and healed and whole,
shining in the reflection of His Love.
In me is His creation sanctified
and guaranteed eternal life. In me
is love perfected, fear impossible,
and joy established without opposite.
I am the holy home of God Himself.
I am the Heaven where His Love resides.
I am His holy Sinlessness Itself,
for in my purity abides His Own.

*h*ere is the only "sacrifice" You ask
of Your beloved Son; You ask him to
give up all suffering, all sense of loss
and sadness, all anxiety and doubt,
and freely let Your Love come streaming in
to his awareness, healing him of pain,
and giving him Your Own eternal joy.
Such is the "sacrifice" You ask of me,
and one I gladly make; the only "cost"
of restoration of Your memory
to me, for the salvation of the world.

father, Your Son is perfect. When I think
that I am hurt in any way, it is
because I have forgotten who I am,
and that I am as You created me.
Your Thoughts can only bring me happiness.
If ever I am sad or hurt or ill,
I have forgotten what You think, and put
my little meaningless ideas in place
of where Your Thoughts belong, and where they are.
I can be hurt by nothing but my thoughts.
The Thoughts I think with You can only bless.
The Thoughts I think with You alone are true.

*W*hatever form temptation seems to take,
it always but reflects a wish to be
a self that you are not. And from that wish
a concept rises, teaching that you are
the thing you wish to be. It will remain
your concept of yourself until the wish
that fathered it no longer is held dear.
But while you cherish it, you will behold
your brother in the likeness of the self
whose image has the wish begot of you.
For seeing can but represent a wish,
because it has no power to create.
Yet it can look with love or look with hate,
depending only on the simple choice
of whether you would join with what you see,
or keep yourself apart and separate.

The savior's vision is as innocent
of what your brother is as it is free
of any judgment made upon yourself.
It sees no past in anyone at all.
And thus it serves a wholly open mind,
unclouded by old concepts, and perpared
to look on only what the present holds.
It cannot judge because it does not know.
And recognizing this, it merely asks,
"What is the meaning of what I behold?"
Then is the answer given. And the door
held open for the face of Christ to shine
upon the one who asks, in innocence,
to see beyond the veil of old ideas
and ancient concepts held so long and dear
against the vision of the Christ in you.

Be vigilant against temptation, then,
remembering that it is but a wish,
insane and meaningless, to make yourself
a thing that you are not. And think as well
upon the thing that you would be instead.
It is a thing of madness, pain and death;
a thing of treachery and black despair,
of failing dreams and no remaining hope
except to die, and end the dream of fear.
This is temptation; nothing more than this.
Can this be difficult to choose *against?*
Consider what temptation is, and see
the real alternatives you choose between.
There are but two. Be not deceived by what
appears as many choices. There is hell
or Heaven, and of these you choose but one.

Let not the world's light, given unto you,
be hidden from the world. It needs the light,
for it is dark indeed, and men despair
because the savior's vision is withheld
and what they see is death. Their savior stands,
unknowing and unknown, beholding them
with eyes unopened. And they cannot see
until he looks on them with seeing eyes,
and offers them forgiveness with his own.

*Y*ou are as God created you. Today
honor your Self. Let graven images
you made to be the Son of God instead
of what he is be worshipped not today.
Deep in your mind the holy Christ in you
is waiting your acknowledgment as you.
And you are lost and do not know yourself
while He is unacknowledged and unknown.

If you remain as God created you,
appearances cannot replace the truth,
health cannot turn to sickness, nor can death
be substitute for life, or fear for love.
All this has not occurred, if you remain
as God created you. You need no thought
but just this one, to let redemption come
to light the world and free it from the past.

In this one thought is all the past undone;
the present saved to quietly extend
into a timeless future. If you are
as God created you, then there has been
no separation of your mind from His,
no split between your mind and other minds,
and only unity within your own.

I am as God created me. His Son
can suffer nothing. And I am His Son.

*t*his holy instant would I give to You.
Be You in charge. For I would follow You,
certain that Your direction gives me peace.

And if I need a word to help me, He
will give it to me. If I need a thought,
that will He also give. And if I need
but stillness and a tranquil, open mind,
these are the gifts I will receive of Him.
He is in charge by my request. And He
will hear and answer me, because He speaks
for God my Father and His holy Son.

Serenity and perfect peace are mine,
because I am one Self, completely whole,
at one with all creation and with God.

father, You have one Son. And it is he
that I would look upon today. He is
Your one creation. Why should I perceive
a thousand forms in what remains as one?
Why should I give this one a thousand names,
when only one suffices? For Your Son
must bear Your Name, for You created him.
Let me not see him as a stranger to
his Father, nor as stranger to myself.
For he is part of me and I of him,
and we are part of You Who are our Source,
eternally united in Your Love;
eternally the holy Son of God.

*h*ow holy are our minds! And everything
we see reflects the holiness within
the mind at one with God and with itself.
How easily do errors disappear,
and death give place to everlasting life.
Our shining footprints point the way to truth,
for God is our Companion as we walk
the world a little while. And those who come
to follow us will recognize the way
because the light we carry stays behind,
yet still remains with us as we walk on.

No miracle can ever be denied
to those who know that they are one with God.
No thought of theirs but has the power to heal
all forms of suffering in anyone,
in times gone by and times as yet to come,
as easily as in the ones who walk
beside them now. Their thoughts are timeless, and
apart from distance as apart from time.

Let me remember I am one with God,
at one with all my brothers and my Self,
in everlasting holiness and peace.

father, our Name is Yours. In It we are
united with all living things, and You
Who are their one Creator. What we made
and call by many different names is but
a shadow we have tried to cast across
Your Own Reality. And we are glad
and thankful we were wrong. All our mistakes
we give to You, that we may be absolved
from all effects our errors seemed to have.
And we accept the truth You give, in place
of every one of them. Your Name is our
salvation and escape from what we made.
Your Name unites us in the oneness which
is our inheritance and peace. Amen.

*W*e thank you, Father, for the light that shines
forever in us. And we honor it,
because You share it with us. We are one,
united in this light and one with You,
at peace with all creation and ourselves.

i walk with God in perfect holiness.
I light the world, I light my mind and all
the minds which God created one with me.

m *y* Self is holy beyond all the thoughts
of holiness of which I now conceive.
Its shimmering and perfect purity
is far more brilliant than is any light
that I have ever looked upon. Its love
is limitless, with an intensity
that holds all things within it, in the calm
of quiet certainty. Its strength comes not
from burning impulses which move the world,
but from the boundless Love of God Himself.
How far beyond this world my Self must be,
and yet how near to me and close to God!

*O*neness is simply the idea God is.
And in His Being, He encompasses
all things. No mind holds anything but Him.
We say "God is," and then we cease to speak,
for in that knowledge words are meaningless.
There are no lips to speak them, and no part
of mind sufficiently distinct to feel
that it is now aware of something not
itself. It has united with its Source.
And like its Source Itself, it merely is.

Into Christ's Presence will we enter now,
serenely unaware of everything except
His shining face and perfect Love. The
vision of His face will stay with you, but
there will be an instant which transcends
all vision, even this, the holiest.
This you will never teach, for you
attained it not through learning. Yet the
vision speaks of your remembrance of
what you knew that instant, and will
surely know again.

*C*hrist's vision has one law. It does not look
upon a body, and mistake it for
the Son whom God created. It beholds
a light beyond the body; an idea
beyond what can be touched, a purity
undimmed by errors, pitiful mistakes,
and fearful thoughts of guilt from dreams of sin.
It sees no separation. And it looks
on everyone, on every circumstance,
all happenings and all events, without
the slightest fading of the light it sees.

This can be taught; and must be taught by all
who would achieve it. It requires but
the recognition that the world can not
give anything that faintly can compare
with this in value; nor set up a goal
that does not merely disappear when this
has been perceived. And this you give today:
See no one as a body. Greet him as
the Son of God he is, acknowledging
that he is one with you in holiness.

Thus are his sins forgiven him, for Christ
has vision that has power to overlook
them all. In His forgiveness are they gone.
Unseen by One they merely disappear,
because a vision of the holiness
that lies beyond them comes to take their place.
It matters not what form they took, nor how
enormous they appeared to be, nor who
seemed to be hurt by them. They are no more.
And all effects they seemed to have are gone
with them, undone and never to be done.

Thus do you learn to give as you receive.
And thus Christ's vision looks on you as well.
This lesson is not difficult to learn,
if you remember in your brother you
but see yourself. If he be lost in sin,
so must you be; if you see light in him,
your sins have been forgiven by yourself.
Each brother whom you meet today provides
another chance to let Christ's vision shine
on you, and offer you the peace of God.

*C**hrist* is God's Son as He created Him.
He is the Self we share, uniting us
with one another, and with God as well.
He is the Thought Which still abides within
the Mind that is His Source. He has not left
His holy home, nor lost the innocence
in which He was created. He abides
unchanged forever in the Mind of God.

Christ is the link that keeps you one with God,
and guarantees that separation is
no more than an illusion of despair,
for hope forever will abide in Him.
Your mind is part of His, and His of yours.
He is the part in which God's Answer lies;
where all decisions are already made,
and dreams are over. He remains untouched
by anything the body's eyes perceive.
For though in Him His Father placed the means
for your salvation, yet does He remain
the Self Who, like His Father, knows no sin.

*father, there is a vision which beholds
all things as sinless, so that fear has gone,
and where it was is love invited in.
And love will come wherever it is asked.
This vision is Your gift. The eyes of Christ
look on a world forgiven. In His sight
are all its sins forgiven, for He sees
no sin in anything He looks upon.
Now let His true perception come to me,
that I may waken from the dream of sin
and look within upon my sinlessness,
which You have kept completely undefiled
upon the altar to Your holy Son,
the Self with Which I would identify.*

Let us today behold each other in
the sight of Christ. How beautiful we are!
How holy and how loving! Brother, come
and join with me today. We save the world
when we have joined. For in our vision it
becomes as holy as the light in us.

111

temptation has one lesson it would teach,
in all its forms, wherever it occurs.
It would persuade the holy Son of God
he is a body, born in what must die,
unable to escape its frailty,
and bound by what it orders him to feel.
It sets the limits on what he can do;
its power is the only strength he has;
his grasp cannot exceed its tiny reach.
Would you be this, if Christ appeared to you
in all His glory, asking you but this:
*"Choose once again if you would take your place
among the saviors of the world, or would
remain in hell, and hold your brothers there."*
For He *has* come, and He *is* asking this.

How do you make the choice? How easily
is this explained! You always choose between
your weakness and the strength of Christ in you.
And what you choose is what you think is real.
Simply by never using weakness to
direct your actions, you have given it
no power. And the light of Christ in you
is given charge of everything you do.
For you have brought your weakness unto Him,
and He has given you His strength instead.

Trials are but lessons that you failed to learn
presented once again, so where you made
a faulty choice before you now can make
a better one, and thus escape all pain
that what you chose before has brought to you.
In every difficulty, all distress,
and each perplexity Christ calls to you
and gently says, "My brother, choose again."
He would not leave one source of pain unhealed,
nor any image left to veil the truth.
He would not leave you comfortless, alone
in dreams of hell, but would release your mind
from everything that hides His face from you.
His holiness is yours because He is
the only Power that is real in you.
His strength is yours because He is the Self
That God created as His only Son.

You *are* as God created you, and so
is every living thing you look upon,
regardless of the images you see.
What you behold as sickness and as pain,
as weakness and as suffering and loss,
is but temptation to perceive yourself
defenseless and in hell. Yield not to this,
and you will see all pain, in every form,
wherever it occurs, but disappear
as mists before the sun. A miracle
has come to heal God's Son, and close the door
upon his dreams of weakness, opening
the way to his salvation and release.
Choose once again what you would have him be,
remembering that every choice you make
establishes your own identity
as you will see it and believe it is.

*Today I let Christ's vision look upon
all things for me and judge them not, but
give each one a miracle of love instead.*

*f*orget not once this journey is begun
the end is certain. Doubt along the way
will come and go and go to come again.
Yet is the ending sure. No one can fail
to do what God appointed him to do.
When you forget, remember that you walk
with Him and with His Word upon your heart.
Who could despair when Hope like this is his?
Illusions of despair may seem to come,
but learn how not to be deceived by them.
Behind each one there is reality
and there is God. Why would you wait for this
and trade it for illusions, when His Love
is but an instant farther on the road
where all illusions end? The end *is* sure
and guaranteed by God. Who stands before
a lifeless image when a step away
the Holy of the Holies opens up
an ancient door that leads beyond the world?

Let us wait here in silence, and kneel down
an instant in our gratitude to Him
Who called to us and helped us hear His Call.
And then let us arise and go in faith
along the way to Him. Now we are sure
we do not walk alone. For God is here,
and with Him all our brothers. Now we know
that we will never lose the way again.
The song begins again which had been stopped
only an instant, though it seems to be
unsung forever. What is here begun
will grow in life and strength and hope, until
the world is still an instant and forgets
all that the dream of sin had made of it.

Let us go out and meet the newborn world,
knowing that Christ has been reborn in it,
and that the holiness of this rebirth
will last forever. We had lost our way
but He has found it for us. Let us go
and bid Him welcome Who returns to us
to celebrate salvation and the end
of all we thought we made. The morning star
of this new day looks on a different world
where God is welcomed and His Son with Him.
We who complete Him offer thanks to Him,
as He gives thanks to us. The Son is still,
and in the quiet God has given him
enters his home and is at peace at last.

*r*eferences for quotations

All references are to the three volumes of *A Course in Miracles (Text, Workbook for Students,* and *Manual for Teachers);* Foundation for Inner Peace, P.O. Box 635, Tiburon, California 94920.

Page 1: *Text,* page 87; *Manual for Teachers,* page 73

Page 2: *Workbook for Students,* page 477

Page 5: *Workbook for Students,* page 396

Page 6: *Text,* pages 602 – 3

Page 7: *Text,* page 549

Page 9: *Workbook for Students,* page 209

Page 10: *Workbook for Students,* page 306; *Workbook for Students,* page 398

Page 11: *Workbook for Students,* page 392

Pages 12 – 13: *Workbook for Students,* pages 334 – 5

Page 14: *Workbook for Students* pages 193 – 4

Page 15: *Workbook for Students,* pages 313 – 4

Page 17: *Workbook for Students,* page 400

Page 18: *Text,* page 570

Page 19: *Workbook for Students,* pages 189 – 90

Pages 20 – 21: *Workbook for Students,* pages 311 – 2

Page 22: *Workbook for Students,* page 393

Page 23: *Workbook for Students,* pages 227 – 8

Page 24: *Workbook for Students,* page 293

Page 25: *Text,* page 571

Pages 26 – 27; *Text,* pages 587 – 8

Page 28: *Workbook for Students,* page 417

Page 29: *Workbook for Students,* page 203; *Workbook for Students,* page 393

Page 30: *Workbook for Students,* page 425

Page 31: *Workbook for Students,* page 395; *Workbook for Students,* page 445

Page 33: *Workbook for Students,* page 206

Page 34: *Workbook for Students,* page 225 – 6

Page 35: *Workbook for Students,* page 182; *Workbook for Students,* page 394

Page 36: *Workbook for Students,* page 419

Page 37: *Workbook for Students,* page 451

Pages 38 – 39: *Workbook for Students,* pages 349 – 50

Page 41: *Workbook for Students,* page 392

Page 42: *Workbook for Students,* page 466

Page 43: *Workbook for Students,* page 432

Pages 44 – 45: *Workbook for Students,* pages 360 – 1

Page 47: *Workbook for Students,* page 380

119

Pages 48 – 49: *Workbook for Students,* pages 347 – 8
Page 50: *Workbook for Students,* page 396
Page 51: *Workbook for Students,* page 406
Page 52: *Workbook for Students,* page 412
Page 53: *Workbook for Students,* pages 183 – 84
Page 54: *Workbook for Students,* page 201; *Workbook for Students,* page 207
Page 55: *Text,* page 518
Page 56: *Workbook for Students,* pages 185 – 6
Page 57: *Workbook for Students,* page 467
Pages 58 – 59: *Workbook for Students,* pages 339 – 41
Page 61: *Workbook for Students,* page 203
Page 62: *Workbook for Students,* page 342
Page 63: *Workbook for Students,* page 448
Page 64: *Workbook for Students,* page 397
Page 65: *Workbook for Students,* page 454
Pages 66 – 67: *Text,* page 617
Page 68: *Workbook for Students,* page 413
Page 69: *Workbook for Students,* page 401
Page 71: *Workbook for Students,* page 205
Page 72: *Workbook for Students,* page 443
Page 73: *Workbook for Students,* page 400
Page 74: *Workbook for Students,* page 399

Page 75: *Workbook for Students,* page 400
Page 76: *Workbook for Students,* page 395
Page 77: *Workbook for Students,* page 341; *Workbook for Students,* page 205
Page 79: *Workbook for Students,* page 208
Pages 80 – 81: *Workbook for Students* page 391
Page 82: *Workbook for Students,* page 437; *Workbook for Students,* page 440
Page 83: *Workbook for Students,* page 473; *Workbook for Students,* page 212
Page 84: *Workbook for Students,* page 355
Page 85: *Workbook for Students,* pages 213 – 5
Page 86: *Workbook for Students,* page 408
Page 87: *Workbook for Students,* pages 358 – 9
Page 89: *Workbook for Students,* page 209
Page 90: *Workbook for Students,* page 454
Page 91: *Workbook for Students,* page 465
Page 92: *Workbook for Students,* page 469; *Workbook for Students,* page 453
Page 93: *Workbook for Students,* page 428
Pages 94–95: *Text,* pages 618 – 9
Page 96: *Workbook for Students,* pages 195 – 6
Page 97: *Workbook for Students,* page 476
Page 99: *Workbook for Students,* page 202

Page 100: *Workbook for Students,* page 416

Page 101: *Workbook for Students,* page 218 – 9

Page 102: *Workbook for Students,* page 338

Page 103: *Workbook for Students,* page 402; *Workbook for Students,* page 288

Page 104: *Workbook for Students,* page 410

Page 105: *Workbook for Students,* page 315

Page 107: *Workbook for Students,* page 290

Page 108 – 109: *Workbook for Students,* page 292

Page 110: *Workbook for Students,* page 421

Page 111: *Workbook for Students,* page 447

Page 112 – 113: *Text,* pages 619 – 21

Page 115: *Workbook for Students,* page 468

Pages 116 – 117: *Manual for Teachers,* pages 87 – 8